Amazing President

THEODORE ROOSEVELT

Mary Dodson Wade

AMAZING AMERICANS

Enslow Elementary

an imprint of

Enslow Publishers, Inc.

40 Industrial Road
Box 398
Berkeley Heights, NJ 07922
USA

http://www.enslow.com

Enslow Elementary, an imprint of Enslow Publishers, Inc.
Enslow Elementary® is a registered trademark of Enslow Publishers, Inc.

Library of Congress Cataloging-in-Publication Data

Wade, Mary Dodson.
    Amazing president Theodore Roosevelt / Mary Dodson Wade.
    p. cm. — (Amazing Americans)
    Summary: "Readers will find out about Roosevelt's life as a young boy through being
president in this entry-level biography"—Provided by publisher.
    Includes index.
    ISBN-13: 978-0-7660-3284-2
    ISBN-10: 0-7660-3284-1
    1. Roosevelt, Theodore, 1858-1919—Juvenile literature. 2. Presidents—United States—
Biography—Juvenile literature. I. Title.
    E757.W136 2009
    973.91'1092—dc22
    [B]
                   2008024892

Printed in the United States of America

10 9 8 7 6 5 4 3 2 1

Photo Credits: John H Trimble, p. 7 (background); Library of Congress, Prints and Photographs Division, pp. 9 (both), 13, 14, 17; Shutterstock, p. 19; Theodore Roosevelt Collection, Harvard College Library, pp. 4, 7 (inset), 10.

Cover Photographs: Theodore Roosevelt, (foreground); Spanish American war scene (background); Library of Congress, Prints and Photographs Division (both)

CONTENTS

CHAPTER 1:
Growing Up 5

CHAPTER 2:
Family Life 8

CHAPTER 3:
President Roosevelt 15

CHAPTER 4:
Roosevelt's Legacy 18

SOMETHING TO THINK ABOUT 20

TIMELINE 21

WORDS TO KNOW 22

LEARN MORE 23

INDEX 24

Growing Up

Theodore Roosevelt was born in New York City in 1858. No one thought the sickly boy would become president one day. Young "Teddy" worked hard to make himself strong. Later, he made the United States strong.

◀ **When Theodore was young, he was often sick.**

Theodore's family was rich. But money could not cure his asthma. His father built a gym in their home. Theodore exercised to get well.

Theodore loved the outdoors. He collected nests, shells, and bones when he visited his summer home on Oyster Bay, New York.

In college, Theodore studied to be a naturalist. Then his father died. His father had helped poor people. Theodore wanted to help people too.

Theodore loved to go outside ▶ and explore Oyster Bay.

6

CHAPTER 2

Family Life

Theodore married Alice Lee. He was happy when she gave birth to a baby girl. But two days later his wife Alice died. Theodore's mother also died the same day as Alice did.

Theodore was too sad to stay in New York. He went out west. He worked hard as a rancher, hunter, and cowboy.

After his wife Alice died, Roosevelt bought a ranch in the Badlands of Dakota Territory.

Alice

Theodore Roosevelt

Two years later he came back. He married Edith Carow. Soon five more noisy children filled their house.

Theodore took charge of the New York City police. He hired new officers. He helped make the city safe.

◄ In December 1886, Theodore married Edith Carow. Here he is with Edith and their children.

Then Theodore worked for the Navy in Washington, D.C. He built new ships to protect our country. He asked men to join the Rough Riders. They fought in a big battle in Cuba and won. That made Theodore famous.

Roosevelt and his "Rough Riders" are photographed on San Juan Hill during the Spanish American War. ▶

CHAPTER 3

President Roosevelt

Roosevelt was elected governor of New York. He ordered business owners to be fair to workers.

Two years later, he was elected vice-president of the United States. Then the President was killed. Theodore Roosevelt became the youngest President.

◀ **Theodore Roosevelt became president in 1901.**

Roosevelt laughed and played games with his children in the White House. The children had many pets. They liked to play tricks. Once, they took a pony upstairs to a bedroom!

Quentin Roosevelt, Theodore Roosevelt's youngest child, is riding his horse on the White House lawn. ▶

CHAPTER 4

Roosevelt's Legacy

Theodore Roosevelt was 60 years old when he died. He was known all over the world. Because of his hard work and courage, the United States became a world leader.

Roosevelt helped create Yosemite National Park. Many people still go there to camp, hike, and enjoy nature. ▶

Something to Think About

Teddy Roosevelt told some school children, "There are two things I want you to make up your mind to do. First, have a good time as long as you live. Next, work hard and do the things you set out to do."

How did he follow those rules?

Teddy Roosevelt said, "My father was the best man I ever knew."

Mr. Roosevelt had built a place for homeless boys and took his own children there each week when he visited them.

How did watching his father affect Teddy's life? Who do you want to be like?

TIMELINE

1858—October 27, born in New York City.

1880—Married Alice Hathaway Lee.

1884—Daughter Alice is born. Wife and mother died.

1886—Married Edith Kermit Carrow.

1895—Head of New York City Police.

1897—Joined Navy Department in Washington.

1898—Formed Rough Riders to fight in Cuba.

Elected governor of New York.

1900—Elected Vice-President of United States

1901—Became president when President McKinley was killed.

1919—January 6, died at Sagamore Hill, Oyster Bay, New York.

☆Words to Know

asthma—An illness that makes it hard to breathe.

elected—Chosen by people who vote.

governor—The head of a state.

national park—A place the government owns to protect animals. Nobody can build houses there.

naturalist—A person who knows about nature.

president—The head of a country.

Rough Riders—Men with horses who went with Theodore Roosevelt to fight in Cuba.

vice-president—The person next in line to be president.

LEARN MORE

BOOKS

McKay, Sindy. *President Theodore Roosevelt*. San Anselmo, CA: Treasure Bay, Inc., 2006.

Schaefer, Lola M. *Theodore Roosevelt*. Mankato, MN: Capstone/Pebble Books, 2003.

INTERNET ADDRESSES

Theodore Roosevelt Association, Oyster Bay, NY

http://www.theodoreroosevelt.org/kidscorner/ trchildrens.htm

Theodore Roosevelt National Park, ND

http://www.nps.gov/thro/

Time for Kids

http://www.timeforkids.com/TFK/specials/articles/ 0,6709,714578,00.html

PLACES TO VISIT

Theodore Roosevelt Birthplace National Historic Site
28 East 20th Street
New York, NY 10003

Sagamore Hill National Historic Site
20 Sagamore Hill Road
Oyster Bay, NY 11771

INDEX

C

Carow, Edith, 11

Cuba, 12

N

New York City, 5, 8

O

Oyster Bay, 6

P

president, 15–16

R

Roosevelt, Alice Lee, 8

Roosevelt, Theodore,
    5–6, 8, 11–12,
    15–16, 18

Rough Riders, 12

V

vice-president, 15

W

Washington, D. C., 12